Mathematical Algorithms *for the*

Day Before Your Coding Interview

Aditya Chatterjee x Ue Kiao

 **OPENGENUS.org**

BE A NATIONAL PROGRAMMER

Mathematics is the central component of Algorithmic Problem solving

Introduction to this Book

This book "**Mathematical Algorithms for the day before your Coding Interview**" is carefully designed to help you get into Problem Solving Mindset for Coding Interview within a day.

We have carefully selected 5 problems which you can complete in a couple of hours. The problems are such that it captures all key ideas of Mathematical oriented algorithmic problems important for Coding Interviews.

With this, you will be able to crack any Coding Interview easily.

We have covered the following problems:

- Smallest number with multiples
- Largest palindrome
- GCD of sub-parts
- Next Permutation

Best of Luck for your Coding Interview.

Book: **Mathematical Algorithms for the day before your Coding Interview**

Series: Day before Coding Interview

Authors (2): Aditya Chatterjee, Ue Kiao

About the authors:

Aditya Chatterjee is an Independent Researcher, Technical Author and the Founding Member of OPENGENUS, a scientific community focused on Computing Technology.

Ue Kiao is a Japanese Software Developer and has played key role in designing systems like TaoBao, AliPay and many more. She has completed her B. Sc in Mathematics and Computing Science at National Taiwan University and PhD at Tokyo Institute of Technology.

Published: 30 May 2020 (1st Edition) – Updated in November 2023.

Publisher: OpenGenus

Contact: team@opengenus.org

Available on Amazon as E-book and Paperback.

Recommended Books

- <u>Linked List Problems</u>: For Interviews and Competitive Programming
- <u>Problems on Array</u>
- <u>Binary Tree Problems</u>
- <u>Dynamic Programming on Trees</u>

- <u>Day before Coding Interview</u> series
- <u>#7daysOfAlgo</u> series

Table of contents

Introduction

Mathematical Algorithms are fundamentally important as several real-life problems can be modeled as a Mathematical problem. Solving such problems require mathematical insights.

These problems are a fundamental part of Interviews as it illustrates the thinking process of the candidate clearly. By going through the problems in this book, you will be well prepared to tackle any Mathematical problem.

Following are some of the problems we have explored which involve ideas to solve a wider range of problems.

- **Smallest number with multiples**

This is a unique problem where we learn key insights regarding Prime factorization, role of primes in multiples and much more.

We improve the time complexity of this problem starting from $O(N^3 * \log N)$ to $O(N * \log N * \log N)$ to $O(N * \log \log N)$.

- **GCD of sub-parts**

This problem brings up key insights involving GCD (a common and important topic) and in the process, we have explored several standard algorithms like Euclidean's GCD Algorithm in the path of developing our custom algorithm for the given problem.

- **Next Permutation**

This problem demonstrates a significant improvement from $O(N^N \times N \times \log N)$ time to $O(N)$ time complexity. Moreover, it illustrates that improving time complexity does not necessarily mean increasing space complexity as it reduces space complexity from $O(N^N)$ to $O(1)$.

This brings in idea of Greedy Algorithms to Mathematical Algorithm and in the process, we have explored several standard algorithms like Heap's Algorithm.

- **Largest palindrome**

In this problem, we have reduced **810000 comparisons** to **~500 comparisons** based on three deep insights. This is a dramatic improvement and demonstrates that even if time complexity cannot be improved, the performance can be improved significantly.

This is a short book designed to bring you in problem solving mindset quickly.

Problem 1: Smallest number with multiples

In this problem, we will find the smallest number that is perfectly divisible (with remainder 0) by all numbers from 1 to N. This is an important problem that brings in insights from how prime numbers are distributed across numbers and role of prime factors in divisibility.

As we solve this problem with 3 incrementally good approaches, we will learn several fundamental ideas like extracting prime factors, generating prime numbers and much more which will prepare you to solve other similar problems.

We will demonstrate 3 approaches to solve this:

- Brute force **O(N³ * log N)**
- Using prime factorization **O(N * log N * log N)**
- Using insights into the problem **O(N * log log N)**

Example to understand the problem better: Consider N = 3, then we need to find a number that is perfectly divisible by 1, 2 and 3. Such numbers are:

and the smallest number is 6.

You will notice that 6 is a multiple of 1, 2 and 3 but this is not true for all N like N = 4.

For N=4, the smallest such number will be 12 which the multiplication of all numbers result in 24.

We will solve this problem with some great insights.

Brute force approach O(N³ * log N)

The brute force approach is to check all numbers until we find a number that is divisible by all numbers from 1 to N.

Now, we can figure out that the solution should be >= N as it should be divisible by N. The maximum number as a solution should be N! which is a simple multiplication of all numbers from 1 to N.

N! can be considered as O(N²). For each number, we must divide by all numbers from 1 to N to check if it is a solution. This process will take O(N logN) for each number.

Thus, the overall time complexity of this problem will be **O(N³ * logN)**.

Pseudocode:

```
int N_factorial = factorial(N);
for(int i = N; i<N_factorial; i++)
    for(int j=1; j <=N; j++)
    {
        if(i%j != 0)
            break;
        if(j == N)
            return i; // our answer
    }
return 0;
```

We have explored the most basic approach. If we use some properties of numbers, we can formulate efficient approaches.

Improved solution O(N * log N * log N)

To understand the basic idea behind this solution, let us analyze the problem at hand at a deeper level. For a given number A, we have the prime factorization as:

$$A = (p_1 \char`\^ j_1) * (p_2 \char`\^ j_2) * ... * (p_m \char`\^ j_m)$$

Where p_i is the ith prime number and j_i is the power of p_i included in A.

For example: $\mathbf{2464 = 2^5 \times 3^0 \times 5^0 \times 7^1 \times 11^1}$

Consider this for all numbers from 1 to N.

Let for a given prime number p_i, each number from 1 to N will have different powers of it within it say $(pw_1, pw_2, ... , pw_n)$.

For our solution S, we need to have as much power of p_i such that it is divisible by all numbers from 1 to N. For this to be possible, we shall take the maximum number from the power set $(pw_1, pw_2, ... , pw_n)$.

We have to do this for all prime factors or prime numbers less that N.

Once we have the maximum power of each prime number, we shall just multiple the prime numbers to the given power to get to our answer.

Generating all primes can be done through a sieve algorithm and it will take **O(N log log N) time**. Choosing the perfect sieve algorithm requires information about the dataset or the value of N. In general, **Sieve of Eratosthenes** works well in practice.

There are **O(log N) prime numbers less than N** and it can take O(log N * log N) time to calculate the prime factorization provided multiplication takes **O(log N) time**.

For each prime number, we can maintain only the largest power and we need to go through all N numbers which will take O(N * log N * log N) to get to our solution.

The time complexity of this approach will be **O(N * log N * log N)**.

Before we dive into the algorithm, let us go through Sieve of Eratosthenes in general. The key idea is that a number is prime only if it is not divisible by any of the primes appearing before it.

With this idea, we start with 2 as a prime number and for every number, we divide the number with every prime number in our list and if none divides it perfectly, we add the number to our prime list. If a number from our prime list divides it, we move to the next number.

The steps are as follows:

- Let prime{} be our set of prime numbers
- Add 2 to prime set
- For every number i for 3 to N
  - If i is divisible by any number in prime set
    - Add i to prime set

There are other algorithms that can find prime numbers with less computations as well. It requires deeper insights like **for a non-prime number N, there should be at least one factor less than $\sqrt{N}$** and other insights.

Pseudocode of Sieve of Eratosthenes:

```
// This function calculates all prime factors
// Sieve of Eratosthenes (in this case)
int sieve (int n)
{
    int a=2;
    for(int i=a; i<=n; i++)
    {
        prime[i] = true;
    }
    for(int i=a ; i*i<=n ; i++)
    {
        if(prime[i] == true)
        {
            for(int j=i*2 ; j<=n ; j=j+i)
            {
                prime[j] = false;
            }
        }
    }
    // move primes to front
    int pos = 0, pos_t = 0;
    for(int i=0; i <= n; i++)
    {
        if(prime[i] != false)
            pos++;
    }
    prime_num = new int[pos];
    for(int i=2; i <= n; i++)
    {
        if(prime[i] != false)
            prime_num[pos_t++] = i;
    }
    return pos; // number of primes
```

```
}
```

As we have the idea of generating prime numbers, let us review the steps of our algorithm:

- Generate all prime numbers less than N
- Maintain a power list which stores maximum power of each prime (default set to 0)
- For each number i from 1 to N
    - find maximum power of each prime number in i
    - If power is greater than the value in our power list, update the list
- Our answer is the product of all prime numbers with power equal to the value in power list.

Following is the pseudocode of our approach:

```
// This function generates the answer
static int smallest_number(int N)
{
    prime = new boolean [N+1];
    int number = sieve(N);
    int smallest_number = 1;

    // To store maximum power count for all prime factors
    int factor[] = new int[number];

    // Go through each number and get power count of prime factors
    for(int j=2; j<=N; j++)
```

```
{
    int j_temp = j;
    for(int i=0; i<number; i++)
    {
        int count = 0;

        // Get maximum power of the prime number in current number j
        while(j_temp % prime_num[i] == 0 && j_temp > 0)
        {
            j_temp = j_temp / prime_num[i];
            count++;
        }

        // Keep track of maximum power
        if(count > factor[i])
            factor[i] = count;
    }
}
for(int i=0; i < number; i++)
{
    smallest_number *= POWER(prime_num[i], factor[i]));
    // POWER(a, b) = a^b
}
return smallest_number; // Our answer
}
```

With insights in the representation of a number in terms of its prime factors, we have improved our solution greatly. The next major improvement is to **improve the way to get the maximum power of a prime number in a number**.

Efficient solution O(N * log log N)

The most efficient solution is to generate all primes less than N and find the maximum power of the prime which is within N and multiple all such prime powers to get the smallest number.

For example, there are M primes less than N.

p1, p2, ... , pm

With this, for each prime p_i, we need to find the maximum power w_i such that:

p_i ^ w_i <= N

The logic in this case is that w_i is the maximum power that can be associated with p_i prime in prime factorization of any number less than or equal to N.

To understand the concept, let us consider this:

- We have N as 30 and 2 is a prime number
- The maximum power of 2 that can appear in all numbers from 1 to 30 is 4 because 2^4 = 16 and 2^5 = 32 which is greater than 30.
- No number between 1 and 30 can have power of 2 as 5

We can find the maximum power as:

$$w_i = FLOOR(\log(N) / \log(p_i))$$

where FLOOR takes the largest integer not greater than the input which can be decimal.

Once we find the power for all such primes, we just need to multiple them to get the smallest number such as:

$$(p_1 \char`\^ w_1) * (p_2 \char`\^ w_2) * ... * (p_m \char`\^ w_m)$$

This is the smallest number which we need. The process of finding the prime numbers can be done using a sieve algorithm which will take **O(N loglog N)** in general.

There will be logN primes in general and finding the power for each will take around O(logN) time if assumed not constant. This results in **O(logN * logN)**.

With this, the time complexity of this approach will be **O(N loglogN)**.

Pseudocode:

```
primes[] = find_primes(N)
smallest_number = 1
for i = 0 to length(primes)
```

```
    p_i = primes[i]
    power = floor(log(N) / log(p_i))
    smallest_number *= (p_i ^ power)
answer = smallest_number
```

With this, we are able to solve this problem efficiently. If you look back, not only did we solved this problem, but also, we gained deep insights about prime factorization of numbers and how we can handle it along with generating prime numbers.

Think of this problem deeply as it unlocks key ideas to solve some of the most challenging number theory problems using Mathematical Algorithms.

Problem 2: GCD of sub-parts

This is a unique and interesting problem as we formulate a Mathematical approach based on a Greedy Algorithm. The brute force approach is exponential in nature ($O(2^N \times N \times \log N)$) which we improve to $O(\sqrt{N})$ which several key insights and explored other related algorithms as well.

Let us explore the problem.

We are given a number N. We need to split it into K unique numbers (let us say A_1, A_2. ..., A_k) such that $A_i == A_j$ only when i == j and sum of them equals N. We need to find these numbers such that GCD of the numbers (A_1, A_2. ..., A_k) is maximum.

This is an **optimization problem**. Mathematically, we can formulate it as:

Split N into K numbers A_1, A_2, ..., A_k such that:

- $A_1 + A_2 + ... + A_k = N$
- $A_i == A_j$ only if i == j
- $GCD(A_1, A_2, ..., A_k)$ is maximum

GCD is the largest number that divides all involved numbers perfect (with remainder 0).

Think of this problem carefully before you go through our problem-solving approach.

We have explored two specific approaches:

- Brute force approach **O(2^N x N x logN)** time
- Optimal approach **O(N) time** complexity
- Further optimization **O($\sqrt{N}$) time** complexity

Brute force Approach

The brute force approach is simple but to formulate requires some basic ideas like:

- How to generate sub-sequences?
- How to calculate Greatest Common Divisor (GCD)?

We will answer both questions as we explore this solution. Following this, we have explored the efficient approach which illustrates the **power of Mathematical insights**.

Let us get started by finding GCD.

We can find the GCD between two numbers using **Euclidean Algorithm**. The time complexity of this approach is **O(log(N))**. The key idea of Euclidean Algorithm is that:

- If A=0 and GCD(A, B) = B
- If remainder of dividing A by B is R, then GCD(A, B) = GCD(B, R).

Let us take an example to understand this further:

Greatest Common Divisor of **285** and **741**

We have to calculate **GCD (285, 741)**

As 285 is less than 741, we need to calculate GCD (741, 285)

GCD (285, 741) = GCD (741, 285)

Now, remainder of dividing 741 by 285 is 171.
Therefore, we need to calculate GCD (285, 171)

GCD (285, 741) = GCD (741, 285) = GCD (285, 171)

Now, remainder of dividing 285 by 171 is 114.
Therefore, we need to calculate GCD (171, 114)

GCD (285, 741) = GCD (741, 285) = GCD (285, 171) = GCD (171, 114)

Now, remainder of dividing 171 by 114 is 57.
Therefore, we need to calculate GCD (114, 57)

GCD (285, 741) = GCD (741, 285) = GCD (285, 171) = GCD (171, 114) = GCD (114, 57)

Now, remainder of dividing 114 by 57 is 0.
Therefore, we need to calculate GCD (57, 0)

As B=0, GCD(57, 0) = 57.

GCD (285, 741) = GCD (741, 285) = GCD (285, 171) = GCD (171, 114) = GCD (114, 57) = GCD (57, 0) = 57

Therefore, Greatest Common Divisor of **285** and **741** is **57**.

With this, you have one of the most common and influential methods to calculate GCD.

Following is the pseudocode of Euclidean algorithm:

```
function gcd(A,B):
   if (A < B):
      return gcd(B,A)
   if (A = 0):
      return B
   return gcd(B, A%B)
```

If we must calculate GCD of N numbers with this approach, we have to do it for two number at a time and it will take N-1 such operations. This will take a complexity of **O(N logN)**.

The steps for brute force approach are:

- Get a list of first N numbers from 1 to N
- Select all combinations of K elements
- For each combination, check the sum. If sum is equal to N, then calculate the GCD and keep track of largest GCD.

To select a combination, you can use binary representation of a number say for a binary representation: 0011000, we have 7 elements and select the 2 elements: 4th and 5th elements.

For N elements, we need to generate binary sequences of N bits and this will take $O(2^N)$ time as there are $O(2^N)$ sequences.

We have explored this technique of sequence generation in detail in this first book of our series "**Day before coding Interview**":

Problems for the day before your coding interview

We have explored other related problems in the book so it is highly recommended you read it to get further knowledge and clarity.

At the same time, if the sequence satisfies the initial conditions of sum to N, then we will calculate the GCD which will take $O(N \log N)$ time as we explored.

This brings the total time complexity to **$O(2^N \times N \times \log N)$**. This is significant.

Optimal Mathematical Algorithm

This is a very powerful approach which involves great insights as this brings the time complexity down from **$O(2^N \times N \times \log N)$** to **$O(N)$ time** which is significant.

First, we will find about how we will get maximum GCD.

By definition, GCD a number **X** is **GCD of (A_1, A_2, ..., A_k)** is that X is factor of all of these numbers.

Hence a number A_i can be written as **$A_i = X * B_i$** (where X is the factor) ... (1)

now since **$A_1 + A_2 + ... + A_k = N$** ... (2)

Now we use (1) in (2) to get:

$$X * (B_1 + B_2 + ... + B_k) = N$$

for X to be maximum, we need to minimize sum of values of B_i.

Since, every number is unique hence every B_i is unique as well.

So, we can easily assume that **$B_1 + B_2 + ... + B_k >= 1 + 2 + 3... + K$**.

$$B_1 + B_2 + ... + B_k >= 1 + 2 + 3 + ... + K$$

Since every value is unique so we assigned least permissible value to everyone.

hence, **$MINIMUM(B_1 + B_2 + ... + B_k) = (K * (K + 1)) / 2 =$ minimum_number**.

so maximum value of X can be N/(minimum_number).

$$MINIMUM(B_1 + B_2 + ... + B_k) = (K * (K + 1)) / 2 = M$$

$$X = N/M$$

but X also has to be an integer, so we can iteratively find the maximum GCD by finding the least number greater than minimum_number which also divides N.

Steps:

- We have N and K
- Calculate **M = K * (K+1) / 2**
- If N < M, we cannot get a solution
- For i from M to N:
    - If N is divisible by i, then our answer is **N/i**

Pseudocode:

```
// function to find maximum GCD
int findMaxGCD(int n, int k) {
   int minimum_number = (k * (k + 1) ) / 2;

   // returning -1 if n can't be split into k unique numbers
   if(n < minimum_number) {
      return -1;
   }
   // the first number that will divide n will give our greatest GCD
   for(int i = minimum_number, i <= n; i++) {
      if(n % i == 0) {
         return n / i;
      }
   }
}
```

Time Complexity is linear O(N) where N is the number.

Note that i ran loop till i equals n so that i get 1 as maximum when nothing else is there (you can take n=6,k=3 for the case)

we can move forward to getting the number's split. now that we found greatest GCD we can surely find the sum of Bi's.

Let it be b.

so, b = n / a

since, B1 + B2 + B3 + ... + Bk = b.

One trivial solution to this is to assign B_1 =1, B_2 =2, till B_{k-1} =k-1,

and B_k = b - (k(k - 1))/2 or B_k= remaining number from sum after assigning others in the given way, this way we maintained uniqueness as well as sum property at same time.

Now you can use (1) to easily find the sequence A_1, A_2, .., A_k.

Further optimization

We can easily optimize this algorithm to $O(\sqrt{N})$ by using complementary property of two numbers.

If x * y = N then x = N / y and one of x or y will be less than or equal to $\sqrt{N}$ and other will be greater or equal to $\sqrt{N}$.

This is an important idea and is applicable to a wide range of problems. Think more on this.

We have optimized the range of for loop in this case.

Optimized pseudocode:

```
// function to find maximum GCD
int findMaxGCD(int n, int k) {
    int minimum_number = (k * (k + 1) ) / 2;

    if(n < minimum_number) {
        return -1;
    }

    int result=0;

    // using complementary number's property
    int i = sqrt(n);
    while(i >= 1) {
        if(n % i == 0) {
            if(i >= minimum_number) {
                res = max(result, n / i);
            }
            if(n / i >= minimum_number) {
```

```
        result = max(result, i);
      }
    }
  }
  return result;
}
```

Time Complexity is **O($\sqrt{N}$)** - since i is going from $\sqrt{N}$ to 1 in the iteration, which optimizes it to great extent.

Hence, we have started with an exponential solution of time complexity **O(2^N x N x logN)** and used several fundamental insights to improve it beyond a linear time algorithm that is to **O($\sqrt{N}$)** time complexity.

Think of the process carefully as it uncovers several key ideas that is used in a wide range of Mathematical problems

---

Problem 3: Next Permutation

Permutations and Selections are a central part of Mathematical algorithms. In our previous problem, we explored how to select K elements out of N elements. This problem deals with the order of N elements. Given a set of elements, we need to find the next order provided all possible order of the elements is sorted.

This is an important problem as it illustrates that it is not necessary that if we increase the space complexity, time complexity will improve. In this problem, by improving the time complexity, we have improved the space complexity in parallel.

Example: Integer Number : **329**

Here, all possible permutation of above integer number are as follows:

```
1] 239
2] 293
3] 329
4] 392
5] 923
6] 932
```

The immediate next smallest permutation to given number of 329 is 392, hence **392 is an next Lexicographic permutated number of 329.**

Think about this problem deeply.

We have solved this using two approaches:

- Brute force approach **O(N^N x N x logN) time** and **O(N^N) space.**
- Efficient approach **O(N) time** and **O(1) space**

Let us understand the size of the search space we are dealing with:

- Given N elements, there are N! permutations.
- If we have a select a certain number of elements from N elements, there will be 2^N combinations.

N! can be approximated as O(N^N).

This is a result of Stirling's approximation.

The exact expression is as follows:

$$N! \sim \sqrt{2\pi N} \times \frac{N^N}{e}$$

Deriving the above expression requires some insights but you will get the basic idea as follows:

- $N! = 1 \times 2 \times \ldots \times N < N \times N \times \ldots \times N = N^N$. Hence, $N! < N^N$.
- If we multiply i^{th} number with $N-i^{th}$ number, then the minimum product is N (for N x 1) and maximum product is $N^2/4$ (for N/2 x N/2). If we consider the maximum product and assume there will be N/2 such multiplications, N! can be approximated as $\frac{N^N}{2^N}$.
- We can arrive at the exact expression starting from the idea that:

$$\log(N!) = \log(1) + \log(2) + \ldots + \log(N) \sim N \log N - N + 1$$

There are several variants of the approximation, but we can safely assume $N! = O(N^N)$.

Note: In computation, N^N is considered as the same class (**exponential**) as 2^N but in general, N^N is slower than 2^N.

Brute force approach

The idea of the brute force approach is simple. We need to generate all possible permutations (order of N elements), sort all permutations and find the next permutation accordingly.

Steps:

- Generate all N! permutations and save them
- Sort all N! permutations
- Go through all permutations one by one and identify the permutation which is our input. Output the next permutation.

The time complexity of this approach is **O(N^N x N x logN)** as:

- There are N! permutations
- Sorting N! permutations will take O(N^N x N log N) time
- N! = O(N^N)

The space complexity is **O(N^N)** as we need to store all N! permutations at the same time.

The key idea is to efficiently generate all permutations.

There are several algorithms to do this but the simplest and the most efficient is Heap's Algorithm which we will go through.

Let us go through the steps of the **Heap's Algorithm** first:

• **Step 1**: First we will calculate the all possible permutation of first N - 1 elements and adding the last element (Nth) to each of these permutations.

• **Step 2**: Iterate the loop starting from 0 till i is less than N, if N is odd, swap the first and last element, and if N is even then, swap the ith element and the last element.

• **Step 3**: In above every iteration the algorithm will produce all the permutations of N elements that end with the current last element.

- **Step 4**: Repeat the steps for all array sizes 1 to N (starting for index 0 always)

Let us go through the pseudocode once:

```
void heapsAlgorithm(unsigned int arr[], unsigned int size) // size is the size of sub-array
{
   // permutation will be displayed when size becomes 1
   if (size == 1)
   {
      displayPermutation(arr);
      return;
   }

   heapsAlgorithm(arr, size - 1);

   for (int i = 0; i < size-1; i++)
   {
      //size is odd, swap first and last element
      if (size % 2 == 1)
           swap(arr[0], arr[size - 1]);
      // size is even, swap ith and last element
      else
           swap(arr[i], arr[size - 1]);
      heapsAlgorithm(arr, size - 1);
   }
}
```

This is a simple yet insightful algorithm.

We have explained this technique intuitively in detail in the first book of our series "**Day before coding Interview**":

Problems for the day before your coding interview

Problems
for the day
before your
coding interview

By Aditya Chatterjee & Ue Kiao

OpenGenus.org

Find it on Amazon: **daybefore1.opengenus.org**

Understanding this algorithm is not simple so we highly recommend you spend some time on this step.

Once you generate the permutations, we need to sort it. You may use any sorting algorithm such as Quick Sort.

Following this, you need to find the next permutation iteratively.

Following is the pseudocode of our brute force approach:

```
set = set of elements

// O(N!) time step
list[] = generate all permutations of set

// Sort all permutations
sort(list)

// Go through each permutation
for permutation in list
    if permutation == set
        then return "Next permutation"
        if there is no next permutation
            then set is the last permutation
```

As the time complexity is exponential $O(N^N \times N \times logN)$, we need to improve it. This is an unique problem as a simple strategy will improve the time complexity to linear O(N).

Efficient Algorithm

The key idea is that between two consecutive permutation in the sorted list of permutation is that few elements from the left side are unchanged while the positions of the elements in the other half is interchanged.

Understanding the pattern is the key to solving this problem efficiently.

Consider a sequence: 0, 1, 2, 5, 3, 3, 0

The next permutation is: 0, 1, 3, 0, 2, 3, 5

If you notice carefully, the left most elements 0 and 1 remains in their original positions.

0, 1, 2, 5, 3, 3, 0

0, 1, 3, 0, 2, 3, 5

The element 2 is moved from 3rd position to 5th position. The key point is which element took the position of 2. It is 3.

The last permutation is always the order where elements are in decreasing order. The next element takes us to the first order where all elements are in increasing order.

Hence, starting from the right side, we need to reverse a part of the list to arrive at the next element.

The idea is to identify the sub-sequence which has elements in decreasing order. The next element to the left (say A) is smaller than the leftmost element of our sub-sequence.

To arrive at the next permutation, we need to replace this element (A) with the smallest element in the sub-sequence which is larger than A (say B).

Hence, we need to swap positions of A and B.

Naturally, the new permutation is larger than the previous permutation but it is not the smallest of its kind. To get the smallest such permutation, we need to sort the elements to the right of B (our sub-sequence) in increasing order.

Recall that our sub-sequence was in decreasing order so to make it in increasing order, we just need to reverse it.

With this, we arrive at the next permutation intuitively.

The steps of this algorithm are as follows:

- **Step 1**: Find the largest index i such that array[i − 1] < array[i] (If no such i exists, then this is already the last permutation.)
- **Step 2**: Find largest index j such that j ≥ i and array[j] > array[i − 1].
- **Step 3**: Swap array[j] and array[i − 1].
- **Step 4**: Reverse the suffix starting at array[i].

Let us go through an example to understand the algorithm further:

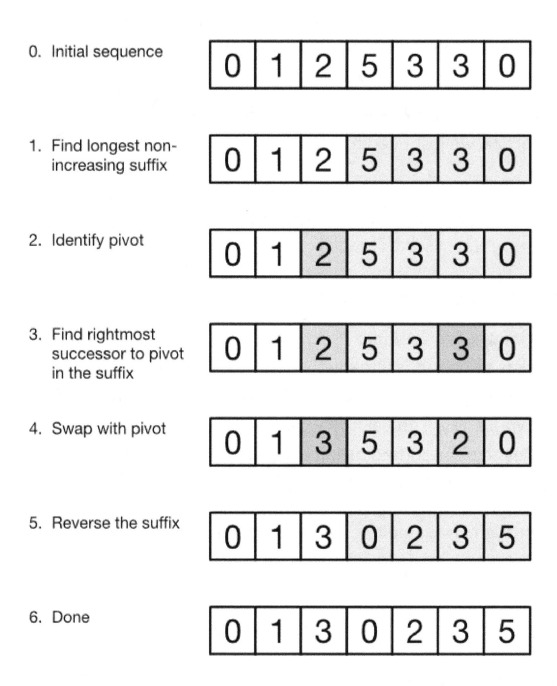

0. Initial sequence   `0 1 2 5 3 3 0`

1. Find longest non-increasing suffix   `0 1 2 5 3 3 0`

2. Identify pivot   `0 1 2 5 3 3 0`

3. Find rightmost successor to pivot in the suffix   `0 1 2 5 3 3 0`

4. Swap with pivot   `0 1 3 5 3 2 0`

5. Reverse the suffix   `0 1 3 0 2 3 5`

6. Done   `0 1 3 0 2 3 5`

In this algorithm, to compute the next lexicographic number will try to increase the number/sequence as little as possible and this will be achieved by modifying the rightmost elements leaving the leftmost elements unchanged.

Here above we have given the sequence **(0, 1, 2, 5, 3, 3, 0)**.

Step 1: Identify the longest suffix that is non-increasing (i.e. weakly decreasing). In our example, the suffix with this property is (5, 3, 3, 0). This suffix is already the highest permutation, so we cannot make a next permutation just by modifying it – we need to modify some element(s) to the left of it. (Note that we can identify this suffix in O(N) time by scanning the sequence from right to left. Also note that such a suffix has at least one element, because a single element substring is trivially non-increasing.)

Step 2: Look at the element immediately to the left of the suffix (in the example it is 2) and call it the pivot. (If there is no such element – i.e. the entire sequence is non-increasing – then this is already the last permutation.) The pivot is necessarily less than the head of the suffix (in the example it is 5). So, some element in the suffix is greater than the pivot. If we swap the pivot with the smallest element in the suffix that is greater than the pivot, then the prefix is minimized. (The prefix is everything in the sequence except the suffix.)

Step 3: In the above example, we end up with the new prefix (0, 1, 3) and new suffix (5, 3, 2, 0). (Note that if the suffix has multiple copies of the new pivot, we should take the rightmost copy – this goes into the next step.)

Step 4: Finally, we sort the suffix in non-decreasing (i.e. weakly increasing) order because we increased the prefix, so we want to make the new suffix as low as possible. In fact, we can avoid sorting and

---

simply reverse the suffix, because the replaced element respects the weakly decreasing order. Thus, we obtain the sequence/ number (0, 1, 3, 0, 2, 3, 5), which is the next permutation that we wanted to compute.

Let us go through the pseudocode:

```
getNextPermutation(array v) // v is input permutation
{
  //find the largest suffix that is non-increasing
  int pos_suffix_start = 0;

  for (pos_suffix_start = v.size()-1; pos_suffix_start > 0 && v[pos_suffix_start-1]
>= v[pos_suffix_start]; pos_suffix_start--);

  // Check if v is the last permutation
  if (pos_suffix_start == 0)
    return "No solution";

  //
  int pos_pivot = pos_suffix_start - 1;

  // find the rightmost digit in suffix that is the
  // least number greater than the pivot, called as swapper.
  int pos_swapper;

  for (pos_swapper = v.size()-1; pos_swapper > pos_pivot && v[pos_swapper] <=
v[pos_pivot]; pos_swapper--);

  //Swap pivot digit with swapper digit
  int tmp = v[pos_pivot];
  v[pos_pivot] = v[pos_swapper];
  v[pos_swapper] = tmp;
```

```
    // Prepare resulting permutation with reversing elements after the pivot digit
    permutation = "";
    for (int i = 0; i <= pos_pivot; i++)
        permutation += v[i];
    for (int i = v.size() - 1; i > pos_pivot; i--)
        permutation += v[i];

    return permutation; // Our answer
}
```

The time complexity of this approach is O(N) which is linear.

This is a significant improvement from **O(N^N x N x logN)** time to **O(N)** time.

Another interesting point is that we are improving the space complexity greatly as well from **O(N^N)** to **O(1)**.

This is a great Mathematical Algorithm, but **can we use it to get better performance than Heap's Algorithm?**

Yes, our algorithm is an insightful algorithm and is mainly, designed for finding the next permutation. You should try its variants like:

- Finding the previous permutation
- Finding the kth permutation

Heap's Algorithm is designed to find all permutations and it has reached the theoretical limit as there are $O(N^N)$ permutations. If we use our algorithm to get permutations one by one, then finding all permutations will take $O(N \times N^N) = O(N^{N+1}) = O(N^N)$ time complexity.

In terms of complexity class, both approaches are the same but in practice:

- Heaps' Algorithm should be used for generating all permutations
- Our Algorithm should be used for generating a restricted set of permutations.

Go through this problem again as it brings up several fundamental ideas in Problem solving.

Problem 4: Largest palindrome

In this problem, we will find the largest palindrome that is a product of two three-digit numbers. In brute force, there are **810000 comparisons** which we have reduced to **~500 comparisons** based on three deep insights. This is a dramatic improvement.

A palindrome is a number where the order of digits is same where it is read from front or back. Example: 104401, 9023209 and so on.

For example: 111111 is a palindrome and is a product of 777 and 143. Similarly, we need to find the largest such palindrome.

Pause and think for a couple of minutes before proceeding further

---

In short, the **insights** are:

- If the two numbers are N1 and N2, then either of them should be **divisible by 11**
- In brute force, we should **start with higher values** of N1 and N2 that is top to bottom
- We need to **check only for N2 < N1** to avoid duplicate checking.
  We will follow a complete flow to understand the insights deeply.

Let us begin with the most basic approach where we will generate all pairs of three-digit numbers and check if the resulting number is a palindrome. From all palindromes, we will keep the largest palindrome.

We can check whether a number is a palindrome or not by creating a reverse of the number by using modulus and multiplication operations.

Pseudocode to check palindrome:

```
palindrome(int N)
{
    int temp = 0, backup = N;
    while(N > 0)
    {
        temp = temp * 10 + N%10;
        N = floor(N/10);
    }
    if (temp == backup)
        return true
    else
        return false
}
```

With the above utility, the brute force approach of getting the largest palindrome is:

```
for i from 100 to 999
    for j from 100 to 999
        int N = i * j
        if(palindrome(N))
            largest = N
 return N
```

Note there are 900 * 900 = **810000 possibilities** to check.

Having a knowledge of the answer, we know that we will arrive at the answer as soon as 993 x 913. In this light, our current approach will make 895 * 900 + 484 = 805500 + 484 = **805984 comparisons**.

Optimization 1

Our first optimization is to start the loop from 999 to 100 instead of 100 to 999. This is because our objective is to find the largest number and if we start from largest three-digit numbers, we may expect to reach the result faster.

In this optimization, it is not clear how many cases are skipped as we do not know the result as of now.

Having a knowledge of the answer, we know that we will arrive at the answer as soon as 993 x 913. Note the first palindrome encountered will be 995 x 583 which is not the largest.

The pseudocode for this technique will be:

```
for i from 999 to 100
    for j from 999 to 100
        int N = i * j
        if(N < largest)
            continue; // skip calculations in 2nd loop
        if(palindrome(N))
            largest = N
```

Note that as soon as we get a palindrome, we are returning it in this case as all further palindromes will be smaller as we will be using smaller sub parts.

This optimization reduces the number of comparisons or computations to **~5000** which is a significant improvement. We can improve it further.

Optimization 2

The idea in this is to avoid duplicate checks. Due to our loop, we are check N1 * N2 and N2 * N1 twice even though the result is same.

To avoid this, we shall begin the second loop from the integer of the first loop. This will reduce the number of comparisons by half overall.

Pseudocode:

```
for i from 999 to 100
    for j from i to 100
        int N = i * j
        if(N < largest)
            continue; // skip pending 2nd loop
        if(palindrome(N))
            largest = N
```

The number of comparisons/ computations in this case is **~4500**.

Optimization 3

This is the major and most insightful optimization.

Our answer (largest palindrome) should have at least 6 digits as we are multiplying 2 three-digit numbers. Let us assume that our answer A has 6 digits and is a palindrome. In this case, it will have 3 unique digits say X, Y and Z.

$$A = 100000 * X + 10000 * Y + 1000 * Z + 100 * Z + 10 * Y + X$$

We can simplify this as:

$$A = 100001 * X + 10010 * Y + 1100 * Z$$
$$A = 11 * (9091 * X + 910 * Y + 100 * Z)$$

Hence, if our answer is 6 digits, it should be a multiple of 11. As 11 is a prime number, either of the two numbers being multiplied should be a multiple of 11.

We must note that our answer must be 6-digit number as both 100 x 100 and 999 x 999 are 6 digit numbers and all other products come in between.

For this, if the outer loop number is not a multiple of 11, then the inner loop must be a multiple of 11 and hence, we can skip several possibilities.

This is an important concept. Think about this deeply 👆

The pseudocode for this technique is:

```
for i from 999 to 100
   if i % 11 == 0
      step = 1
   else
      step = 11
   for j from i + 11 - i%11 to 100 in increment of step
      int N = i * j
      if(N < largest)
         continue;
      if(palindrome(N))
         largest = N
```

Note that i + 11 - i%11 is the number just greater than i which is a multiple of 11.

The number of comparisons in this case is **<500** which is dramatically reduced from the initial value.

This is a simple problem, but it shows how simple incremental improvements greatly optimize a solution. This prepares you to handle mathematical problems correctly.

We just solved an algorithmic problem by exploring central ideas in basic Number Theory handling. Enjoy 👌

Concluding Note

With this, we have come to the end. You should think of the problems we have explored and try to come up with solutions to variants of the problems like:

- Find Kth largest permutation of a List
- Find the previous permutation of a List
- Smallest palindrome from the product of 2 three-digit numbers
- Smallest number with multiples of every even number between 1 and N
- GCD of three numbers
- Maximize GCD by removing an element

and much more.

You may implement the solutions we presented in the programming language you are comfortable in as well. This will strengthen your concept.

Keep learning and solving computational problems

Feel free to get in touch with us and enjoy learning and solving computational problems.

For gaining more experience, you can join our Internship program:

internship.opengenus.org

www.ingramcontent.com/pod-product-compliance
Lightning Source LLC
LaVergne TN
LVHW081805050326
832903LV00027B/2109